NATIONAL LAMPOON'S®

WHITE BREAD
SNAPS

a parody

CB

CONTEMPORARY
BOOKS

A TRIBUNE NEW MEDIA COMPANY

Library of Congress Cataloging-in-Publication Data

National lampoon's white bread snaps.
        p.   cm.
    ISBN 0-8092-3256-1 (alk. paper)
    1. American wit and humor.   2. Invective.   I. National lampoon.
II. Contemporary Books, inc.
PN6231.I65N37   1995
818'.540208—dc20   95-24387
                                                        CIP

This book is dedicated to the retarded guy who works at Carl's, Jr.

Cover photo © 1995 by Michael Slaughter
Interior photos by Mario Cavazos

Published by Contemporary Books, Inc.
Two Prudential Plaza, Chicago, Illinois 60601-6790
Manufactured in the United States of America
International Standard Book Number: 0-8092-3256-1
10   9   8   7   6   5   4   3   2   1

They came to my home and asked
Can you recommend a governess?
I said, Yes, your mother;

They inquired further,
Is is true that the British . . .
I said, Ask your mother;

And they queried me on Sunday,
Which is the way to the Easter service?
I said, Ask your mother;

That makes a man white—
Wine and song and playing the dozens.

—Henry Wadsworth Longfellow V
Poet Laureate

Contents

Foreword

An Introduction to the Art of the Dozens

By William F. Buckley VI

Like CNN, the vodka martini, and Scrabble, white bread snapping—also referred to as "playing the Caucasian dozens"—derived out of cultural necessity. It is an advanced sociological condition that, similar to golf, allows for a conversion of pain to joy. The white man's blues, so to speak. The object of playing the dozens is, of course, to keep snapping until one's opponent backs down, runs out of snaps, or phones his attorney.

Exactly where this traditional art form originated is a topic of considerable debate. Most assume it spawned from the raw, hard-core ghetto known as the Harvard freshman dormitory. Others claim that white bread snapping came from Europe. The latter argument could perhaps be evidenced in this early, never-before-published quote from Shakespeare, which has the stripped-down feel of a modern-day snap:

"Your love is so fickle, only tender churl mak'st waste as the fair wench should by time decease."

Though the snap translates poorly into today's world, back then it was regarded as uproarious.

Either way, playing the Caucasian dozens is intrinsic to our conservative culture. It is necessary, though, for people to be educated in the effective use of white bread snapping as a tool for disarming potentially "sticky" situations. I can only draw from personal experience to illustrate.

One crisp November morning, my less-than-ambitious nineteen-year-old son showed up unexpectedly at my New Canaan home. With great apathy, he proceeded to explain to Constance and me how he had been asked to leave Barnstable Preparatory School as a result of his illicit behavior involving a controlled substance and unreasonably frequent demands for access to his trust fund. Well, Constance and I were aghast but not entirely surprised. After all, we're talking about the same lad who a year prior was dismissed from his prom for drinking schnapps, only to completely demolish his mother's Pathfinder on the way home. I was at the end of my rope, and I let him know it. I called him an embarrassment to the family and told him to take his trust fund and get the "h-e-double-hockey-sticks out."

He turned to leave, but just as he reached the door, a curious thing happened. I suppose I had pushed him too far, and in his lament he had recalled the age-old Caucasian dozens credo: If you can't think of something nice to say, say something mean instead.

He kicked off his loafers, cocked himself up to his full height, and assumed the "dozens stance" his godfather had taught him when he was in the nursery. I was a bit taken aback, but I admired his moxie and did little to stop him, other than to put down my Chivas Regal and remove my cardigan. It was man time.

As would any good snapper, he understood the

importance of maintaining a cool exterior. But his eyes radiated with a crazed, chilling intensity. Growing up the smallest child in a large Republican family had given him a "no fear" attitude that helped him to overcome his lack of size (5'2"). He had even made the lacrosse team at Barnstable. Now, though, the stakes were far higher. He rose to the occasion, bless him, belting out droll and penetrating, but mostly droll, words that exploded in my eardrums like miniature hand grenades. These were not the snaps that I had taught him. These snaps were, to put it bluntly, quite harsh—"color snaps," "age snaps," "financial snaps"—even "mother" snaps, which I thought showed particular gumption, as Constance was standing in the room at the time.

Not to be outdone, I promptly fired back some of my best snaps—snaps that mocked his posture and his slovenliness. I even "busted" a snap about the consequences of "size being bricks" or something to that effect.

Forty-five minutes later, we two men were arm in arm,

tears of laughter streaming down our cheeks and the sweetly pungent hum of fraternity in the air. Constance breathed a sigh of relief and I "got busy" on the phone with the Barnstable Dean of Admissions.

I hesitate to consider the outcome had we not been able to call upon our WASP heritage for a good, old-fashioned battle of mean-spiritedness—mano a mano. And that is the blessing of white bread snaps—it allows us to roll up our sleeves and settle our differences the old-fashioned way—by fighting with our wits, not our attorneys. Granted, snapping is not to everyone's taste. But as the maxim goes: "If we can't laugh at ourselves, who can we laugh at?" Other people, I suppose.

—William F. Buckley VI
Martha's Vineyard

Acknowledgments

Thanks to all the white bread people who made this book possible—especially Jim Jimirro, the whitest of them all.

Specific thanks also go to the following people, all of whom can snap even better than we can: Curtis Anderson, Kenny Sutherland, B. B. King, Tino Magnatta, Gino from traffic school, Vic Barone, Hillary Clinton, Michael Lauer, Gene Grey, Bil Dwyer, Bill Torres, Jen Mosberg, J. T., John Hayes, Cheryl Bloome, Charlotte Hassett, Woody Fraser, Sam Gross, Dennis Hopper, Mary Dixie, Corrine, David Weinstein, Cindy Schultzel, Mike Weiss, Nancy, the Adelmeister, David Teitelbaum, Tara Zanecki, Zachmaster Flash and the Furious Sam, Mario, Fernando, Mike Waeghe, Dean Christopher, Jeff Labounty, Chet Cooper, Howard Labe, Nina Hann, Patty Jackson, Chris Barnes, Tom Stern, Stuart Shapiro, Eric Goldberg, Tracey Quelch, Mike Delucca, Neal Israel, Adam Kline, Amy Bomse, Duncan Murray, Ben Ho, Nick D'Angelo, Jennifer Siegal, Mary Catherine, Joel Ball, Shawn Furst, Hikaru, Ian, Glen, all the guys at Electromedia, David Bowers, Louis Gossett, Steven Bernstein, Woodward, Chuy, Mary Kimmel, Derrick Barney, Ken Rosenblood, Sharon Feldman, Jennifer Hughes, Steve Kahn, the boy with one kidney, Mike the Surfer, the Fresh Prince of Darkness, the lady at Arby's, Carrot Top, Joe DeBartolo, Guy Hammond, Jeff Pill, Todd David Schwartz, Rhonda Shear, Chief Eagle Eye, Tom Campbell, Fantastic Man, Lopez, Peter Ackroyd, Dick Crystal, Dick Miller, Chris Miller, Miller Daniel, Daniel Butnick, You're Gonna Die, the retarded guy who works at Carl's, Jr., and the entire Bush administration.

Introduction

White bread snapping, our sources tell us, has spread beyond private-school playgrounds and into board meetings, Latin-club picnics, and debutante balls across the nation. A fixture of better cocktail parties, white bread snapping has also appeared in such diverse arenas as Michael Bolton albums and the Senate floor.

White bread snapping is a hit, and for good reason. Who doesn't savor the satisfaction of putting that special someone in his or her place—whether it's the senior partner in your Upper East Side law firm or that graduate economics professor at your exclusive Ivy League university?

It is, of course, the stinging punch line of a good white bread snap that makes playing the Caucasian dozens so satisfying. The game, however, should be played with care—not everyone has a sense of humor. To play the game with those sensitive, serious types, you might want to consult the "Extremely Harsh Snaps" chapter—after all, if it's inevitable that your victim will be offended, you might as well go all the way. It's also a good idea to have some lunch money on hand in case you need to buy back your front teeth. Have fun, my man!

P.S. If comic books interest you, we suggest you take a look at our own snapping superhero in "The Amazing Adventures of the Enigmatic Snapsmith" in the back of the book.

NATIONAL LAMPOON®

FAT SNAPS

You are so fat, you frequently have to **stop and catch your breath** during aerobics classes.

Your mother is so fat that in high school she had **trouble getting dates.**

Your brother is so fat that he has to shop at the "big and fat" store.

YOUR MOTHER IS SO LARGE,

SHE COULD PLAY THE LEAD IN THAT WAGNER "RING CYCLE" OPERA.

YOUR SISTER IS SO **FAT** SHE CAN'T FIT INTO **ANYTHING**, IN THE J. CREW CATALOG.

Your godmother is so gluttonous, she once ate an entire quiche lorraine **in one sitting.**

If fatness were bricks, your brother would have plenty.

Your sister is so fat, she looks like **some kind of an animal.**

YOUR MOTHER IS SO FAT THAT SHE MUST WEIGH A TON. WELL NOT LITERALLY, BUT IT MUST BE A LOT.

Your sister has to purchase two first-class seats on Virgin Atlantic Airways when she flies to London because she is so fat.

If cellulite were fat, your mother would have it **on her legs**.

Your girlfriend wears a **size XXL** sweatshirt.

STUPID
SNAPS

Your brother is so stupid, he flew to Switzerland to buy a **fake Rolex.**

Your mother is so stupid, she once had **too much to drink** at the country club and gave the valet a ten-dollar tip.

Your father is so stupid, **he once chilled** red wine and served it to Orientals.

If stupidity were bricks, your mother would have plenty.

Your father is so stupid, I saw him wearing white slacks **after Labor Day.**

If stupidity were a shag carpet, you would win the Nobel Peace Prize.

Your mother is so stupid, she thought *Moby-Dick* was written by Charles Dickens.

Your great-grandmother is so stupid, she died many years ago of emphysema, caused (probably) by years of smoking.

Your brother is so stupid, he showed up at my sister's coming-out party in a **tweed jacket.**

YOUR SISTER IS SO STUPID THAT SHE HAD DIFFICULTY WITH HER SATs.

Your brother is so dumb, he went to Yale because he thought New Haven would be a **"great place to live."**

Your husband is **so absent-minded**, he once dropped you off at preschool and your five-year-old daughter at the AA meeting.

Your father is so stupid, he pays high malpractice insurance.

Your sister is a dumb-ass.

UGLY
SNAPS

If ugliness were bricks, **your mother** would have quite a few of them.

You are so ugly that if ugliness were measured on a scale, you would be way off it, or at least near the end.

You are so ugly that people often refer to you as **"unsightly."**

YOUR FATHER IS SO **UGLY** THAT THEY TOOK HIS PICTURE **OUT** OF THE STANFORD ALUMNI BOOK, DESPITE HIS GENEROUS **DONATIONS.**

You are so ugly, **you never get any** modeling jobs.

Your son is so unattractive, he once dated a Jewish girl **for eight months** without fornicating.

Your little sister is so ugly, she is never molested by your overbearing father, who appears to the world to be loving and well adjusted.

YOUR BROTHER
IS SO UGLY, HE THOUGHT MULTIVITAMINS WOULD IMPROVE HIS COMPLEXION, BUT THEY DIDN'T.

BIG
SNAPS

Your bank account is so big, you rarely have to balance your checkbook.

Your buttocks are so large, the doctor has trouble **injecting you** with antibiotics.

Your father's house is so big, he had to hire **additional servants.**

If bigness were bricks, you would have some pretty big bricks.

YOUR **STEPMOTHER'S** **LINCOLN** **CONTINENTAL** **IS SO BIG, SHE** **CAN'T** **PARALLEL** **PARK** **LIKE SHE COULD WHEN SHE OWNED A SMALLER, MORE SENSIBLE LEXUS.**

THE **MOLE** ON YOUR MOTHER'S **BACK** IS SO **BIG,** THE DERMATOLOGIST RECOMMENDED SHE HAVE IT REMOVED (OR WATCH IT VERY CAREFULLY TO SEE IF IT TURNS BLACK OR GREEN, WHICH WOULD SIGNIFY A POSSIBLE MALIGNANCY).

SMALL
SNAPS

Your sister's butt **is so small**, men find it attractive.

Your father's trust fund is so small, he had to teach an additional class this semester to **"help make ends meet."**

You are so small that you could be a **racehorse jockey.**

You're so small from dieting that you **had to buy** new clothes.

Your breakfast nook is so tiny that you have to eat **miniature sausages** with your crepes.

If smallness were bricks, you would have some **very small bricks.**

Your college condominium is so small, you **had to have it redecorated** in order to make it livable.

Your summer villa is so small, your **extended family** has to plan two trips in order to accommodate everyone.

Your sister is so small, **when she sits** in the back seat of a Bentley, her feet dangle.

YOUR
TRUST
FUND IS SO SMALL,
YOU CAN'T AFFORD
TO GO TO EUROPE
THIS YEAR.

Your father's appetite is so diminutive, he once took two bites out of a filet mignon and said, "Anybody want the rest of this?"

Your gardener's vocabulary is so small, I asked him to extricate the geraniums from my garden and he looked at me with puzzled, swarthy little eyes.

Your family room is so small, when I was shooting at the eight ball, my cue stick **knocked against the wall.**

TEETH AND MOUTH SNAPS

If teeth were bricks, you would have many bricks. However, if a mouth were a brick, **you would have just one.**

You haven't **worn your retainer** in so long, your teeth are crooked again.

You don't use **tartar-control toothpaste** all the time, so the dentist has to scrape a lot when you go in for checkups.

You wore braces.

YOUR TEETH NEED BONDING.

SMELLY
SNAPS

You smell so bad that you require a **bath**.

Your sister's perfume smells like one of those **imitation ones** that you purchase from the guys who come around your office building once a month and usually get chased away by the building manager.

Jesus, man, have you been drinking?

IF SMELL WERE BRICKS, YOU WOULD HAVE PLENTY.

OLD
SNAPS

Your grandfather is so old that he **collects Social Security** on a monthly basis.

If age were bricks, you would have some **very old bricks.**

Your Rolls Royce is so old, it doesn't have the **mandatory driver's-side** airbag.

YOUR GRANDMOTHER IS SO OLD THAT SHE IS YELLOW AND CRACKED LIKE THE DECLARATION OF INDEPENDENCE.

Your mother is so old, she not only remembers President Nixon but voted for him as well.

You look very old, whereas I look youthful.

The wine in your cellar **is so old** that you really ought to consider it an investment.

Is your daughter Penelope **eighteen** yet?

POOR
SNAPS

Your mother is so poor that when she **tipped her masseuse** she asked for a receipt.

Your family is so poor that when you **vacationed in the islands** your father said, "Now let's not go crazy with the room service, kids."

Your father is so poor, he rarely skis in Switzerland anymore.

Your mother is so poor, she had to ask the **divorce-court judge** for additional alimony from your father.

If poorness were bricks, you would have plenty.

Your father was **running low on funds,** so he had to dip into his client trust account (illegally, I might add).

YOU ARE SO POOR THAT YOU CAN'T BUY THINGS THAT YOU NEED MUCH LESS WANT.

You are so poor that you're on financial aid.

Your parents are so poor, they can't afford to send both **you and your sister** to an Ivy League university.

Your sister is so poor, she spent spring break **in Connecticut** with your family.

YOUR MOTHER IS **SO POOR** THAT SHE BOUGHT A CAR AND HAD TO MAKE PAYMENTS ON IT.

DIRTY
SNAPS

You're so dirty that, quite frankly, I wouldn't be surprised if you hadn't showered in a long time.

Your immediate family is so filthy that sometimes they aren't allowed to eat at fine restaurants.

If dirt were bricks, you would have lots.

Your son is so nasty, that head-lice epidemic at his prep school was largely attributed to him.

Your house is so dirty, your father had to call a **maid service.**

Your fingernails are so dirty, people might think **you have to work** for a living.

YOUR GUEST COTTAGE IS SO NASTY, I FOUND COFFEE-MUG STAINS ON THE KITCHEN COUNTER.
(EVER HEARD OF COASTERS, ASSHOLE?)

SKINNY
SNAPS

If skinniness were bricks, you would have plenty.

Your sister is so skinny, she uses other people's fingers to **gag herself** with.

Your father is so skinny that people at the country club refer to him as "that skinny guy" or "that thin man."

EAR/NOSE/ THROAT SNAPS

Your ear/nose/throat are so **inflamed from an infection,** you had to go to a specialist.

If ear/nose/throat were bricks, you would have **all four together.**

Your sister's ear/nose/throat **are so large,** when she sneezes she often startles small children.

BODY
SNAPS

If eyes were bricks, you would have two.

If hands were bricks, your bricks would need a manicure.

If your whole body were made of bricks, you'd be in trouble. None of your vital functions would work—for example, the heart's blood-pumping function.

CAUCASIAN SNAPS

You are so white, you got a **third-degree burn** on your first day of vacation in the islands.

You are so Caucasian that you think **Michael Bolton** is really soulful.

If color were bricks, you'd have one white brick, because you're white.

YOU'RE SO WHITE
I'D SWEAR THAT YOU WERE AN
ALBINO
(IF IT WEREN'T FOR YOUR
BROWN EYES).

SEX SNAPS

IF **SEX** WERE BRICKS, YOU MIGHT OR **MIGHT NOT** HAVE BRICKS TONIGHT.

When it comes to sex, **your sister is** like a mattress—rectangular, covered with sheets, and stuffed with down.

Your father's penis is so tiny, after he plays squash with the guys he pretends he's late for an appointment so he **doesn't have to shower** with them.

Your girlfriend is **so depraved** that she has sex with you on a daily basis.

If sex were made **an Olympic event,** a lot of people would be really surprised.

Your wife has sex so much, she had to go on **birth control.**

Your parents had sex. That's how you were conceived.

YOUR SISTER
PUT SOMEONE'S
FILTHY PENIS IN HER
MOUTH
(OR SO I HEARD).

FINANCIAL SNAPS

If all **investors** were risk averse, you would never sell any securities.

Your T-bills are **so overvalued,** you should take a capital loss.

Your portfolio is so undiversified, it fluctuates **with the S & P Index.**

Your bonds are rated **C.**

Your junk bonds are so unstable, even **risk-taking individuals** refuse to purchase them.

Your currency **is so inflationary,** no one in your country opens time-deposit accounts.

If capital losses were bricks, you would have plenty.

YACHTING
SNAPS

IF YACHTS WERE BRICKS, YOURS WOULD SINK.

Your **chances of winning** the America's Cup are so slim, you'd best withdraw from the race.

Your father's dinghy is so small, he **needs tweezers** to lower it.

Your yacht is **so underequipped**, it would probably never finish the regatta.

Your spinnaker **is so loose**, it screws the wind.

My anchor is like your wife—wet, heavy, and **permanently tied** to my dinghy.

Jesus, man, have you been drinking?

U.S.S. ENTERSNAPS

If ugliness were photon torpedoes, you could **blow a hole** in a passing vessel's force field.

You're so strange, you're **like a Vulcan** with smooth, round ears.

You have the personality of a Romulan and the **sex life** of a Klingon.

The coordinates you give are so inaccurate, **we usually end up** in the Neutral Zone.

You are so illogical, you become emotional upon **hearing of the death** of your entire family.

If Tribbles were bricks, you would have plenty.

YOU ARE SO HORNY, YOU'D FRENCH KISS AN ALIEN WOMAN FROM ANOTHER PLANET.

Your sister is so stupid, an infant Vulcan is too smart to mind-meld with her.

Your mother is so ugly, randy Klingons **refuse to mate** with her.

If stupidity were **dilithium crystals,** you could power the ship at Warp Four.

SCOUT
SNAPS

If they gave merit badges **for ugliness,** you would have one.

Your clove hitch is so nappy, it looks like you **got a noose** around Buckwheat's head.

Your circle jerk is $2\pi r$.

YOU ARE SO **STUPID,** YOU THOUGHT THERE WAS A SKILL AWARD FOR MASTURBATION.

Your erection is so powerful, the troop **throws a blanket** over you and calls it a tent.

Your children are so ugly, the scout-master refuses to fondle them.

The knots you tie are so inadequate, **the family your troop kidnapped** last weekend escaped after being tied and left for dead in the mountains.

MEDIEVAL SNAPS

Thrice did ye father seeketh out forgiveness, and thrice did the Pope **rejecteth his plea.**

Five maidservants and four eunuchs doth it take to **remove thy mother** from the bed.

If fat had the qualities of hay, bovine creatures would partake of your mother.

Ye sister is **so loose**, even the eunuchs take their turn with her.

Ye mother is so stricken with the plague, **not even lepers** will touch her.

Forsooth, if thine protests **were bricks**, ye wouldst have too many bricks.

DAUGHTERS OF THE AMERICAN REVOLUTION SNAPS

Your great-great-great-great-grandfather was **such a coward,** he shot when he saw the Redcoats' white shirts.

Samuel Adams was so ugly, the Boston Tea Party was **the only time** he ever got his dick wet.

Your great-great-great-grandfather's penis **was so tiny,** they refused to accept his John Hancock on the Declaration of Independence.

WHEN **PAUL REVERE** SAID, "THE BRITISH ARE COMING," HE **MEANT** IN YOUR GREAT-GREAT-GREAT-GREAT-GRANDMOTHER'S **MOUTH.**

BEVERLY HILLS SNAPS

You are so stupid, you don't know how to pronounce Rodeo.

You drive a 1993 Bentley.

When you have lunch at Morton's, the **waiters snicker** at you behind your back.

YOU OUT ARE SO OF THE CLUB SCENE THAT YOU HAVE TO STAND IN LINE AT THE VIPER ROOM.

DAIRY
SNAPS

Your cow is so nasty, she gives **chocolate milk**.

Your Guernsey is **so ugly**, even her calves refuse to suck her udder.

You're so nasty, you sold bull's milk to the co-op.

You're so stupid, you bought Stairmasters for your Jerseys so you could have **low-fat milk**.

EATING DISORDER SNAPS

You're so skinny, when you forced yourself to **vomit over the commode,** you accidentally flushed yourself.

You say you're training for the **marathon**, but you're actually training to become the human javelin.

If vomit were bricks, **you'd have a lot** of bricks to clean up.

Are you gonna eat that?

YOU ARE **ANOREXIC,** THAT'S TRUE, BUT YOU WOULD LOOK PERFECT IF YOU LOST ONLY FIVE MORE POUNDS.

VIVE LES SNAPPZ

You are so culturally inferior, your **knowledge of art** is questionable.

You're so stupid, you actually stood your ground **when the Germans invaded.**

Your mother is so fat, they had to drop the guillotine blade twice to chop **through her neck.**

You're so nappy, they call you Napoléon.

VIVA LOS SNAPOS

You are so lazy that when they said fiesta, you thought they said siesta, so **you went to sleep.**

Your village is **so poor,** your piñatas are filled with rocks.

Your mother's beans are so gaseous, **they could fuel** your low-rider.

You lost your green card.

LAND OF THE RISING SNAP

Your father is so honorable, he can't **sneak attack** a sleeping naval base.

Your mother is **so dishonorable,** she chopped off her father's head.

You are so buck-toothed, foreign competitors **laugh in your face.**

You are so shameful, Buddha wreaks havoc on your Shinto shrine.

YOUR **WORKPLACE** IS SO INEFFICIENT, MOST EMPLOYEES TAKE **ONE HOUR** FOR **LUNCH.**

You are so poor, **you have only** two cameras.

Your father is **so dumb,** he felt an earthquake and thought it was Godzilla.

You are **so buck-toothed,** samurai sharpen swords in your mouth.

Your ancestors drank **cheap rice wine.**

CONGRESSIONAL
SNAPS

Your bill is so stupid, I'll not even consider voting for it.

That congressional page **is so ugly,** he probably won't ever be sodomized this term.

Your **congressional district** is so poor, I wouldn't vote for redistricting it.

Your congressman **is so left,** he jerks off in Maryland and ejaculates in Virginia.

KENNEDY
SNAPS

You're such a **bad swimmer,** even Mary Jo Kopechne could beat you in the breaststroke.

You're so skinny, even Sirhan Sirhan couldn't hit you at **point-blank range.**

You have so much dandruff, even rifle shots from rogue CIA agents couldn't penetrate your skull.

MARLIN PERKINS'S WILD SNAPDOM

(ANIMAL SNAPS)

The **toucan's legs** are like butter—smooth and easy to spread.

The python's dick is **so small**, it looks like a wrinkled tic-tac in the grass.

The armadillo is the buffet of the animal kindgom—everyone can help themselves.

The manatee is so fat, **she uses a** satellite dish as a diaphragm.

IF UGLINESS WERE BRICKS, THE LUNGFISH WOULD BE A HOUSING PROJECT.

The panda is so fat, it uses a hula hoop **as a bracelet.**

The Komodo dragon is **so skinny,** it uses a rubber band as a belt.

That shark is so toothless, it takes him **an hour to eat** a Santa Cruz surfer.

SNAPPER JOHN, M.D.
(MEDICAL SNAPS)

Your liver is so inflamed, we have to give you a **transplant**.

If cholesterol **were bricks,** you'd have plenty.

Your arteries are so clogged, we have to do angioplasty.

You've got the **largest prostate** in the tristate area.

Your heartbeat is so weak, we have to **shock you** with the fibrillator.

If cholesterol were testosterone, you could sleep with every woman in the state.

Jesus, man, have you been drinking?

THE ONLY DIFFERENCE
BETWEEN YOUR SISTER
AND THE LUMP
I FOUND IS THAT YOUR SISTER'S
NOT MALIGNANT.

EXTREMELY HARSH SNAPS

Your mother has so many yeast infections that she could assist in the making of **various baked goods.**

If feathers were **guacamole,** you could fly.

Your mother **just died** in a car accident.

I'm sure you've lost your mind. Just **look at yourself.**

You're making a **fool of yourself,** and you're embarrassing me!

Jesus, man, have you been drinking?

Get hold of yourself.

Just leave me alone.

YOU
SUCK.

MOVES AND STANCES FOR WHITE BREAD SNAPPING

◀Handshake Parley

A trick move developed by European snappers to give one's opponent a false sense of security. This is often a prelude to a gradual escalation of snap hostilities or to an all-out snapkrieg.

The Harangue Dis▶

A snap designed to instill in an opponent an inferiority complex based on the performance of his portfolio compared with that of the Dow-Jones Industrials. A psychologically devastating maneuver.

◀The "What Did I Do to Deserve This" Defensive Stance

This posture indicates displeasure at a perceived unwarranted attack.

Sound Wave Collection Gesture▶

Popularized by scientists at Bell Laboratories during their daily snap festivals, this gesture is used to hear the "dope" snaps from their more soft-spoken brethren.

◀Index Revelatory Stance

Gives snaps added comic emphasis by driving one's index finger straight toward the embattled heart of one's opponent. Especially humorous if delivered in front of a large crowd of family members.

The "T-for-Time" Stall Dis ▶

This tactic is used to control the tempo of the match and give a beleaguered snapper time to think of an appropriate course of action. First employed by Davy Crockett during "The Great Tennessee Snap Debate."

◀Hush Money Maneuver

The truth hurts, especially when everybody knows about it. Protecting one's reputation is paramount. To prevent word from getting out, money must be paid.

The Cooney Surprise, a.k.a. the Cold-Cock Rebuttal▶

Not officially recognized by the Snaps Rules Committee, this move was popularized by the gritty urban ne'er-do-wells of Westchester County during the Snap-Freestyle Movement of the late '60s.

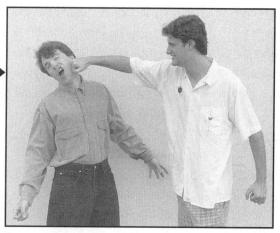

The Rocky Retort ▶

This snap was first
displayed by Rocky Balboa,
the greatest snapper the
world has ever seen,
during his first title defense
against that guy who later
appeared in the movie
Action Jackson.

THE ADVENTURES OF THE ENIGMATIC SNAPSMITH

WHEREVER EVIL REARS ITS HIDEOUS HEAD, ONE CAUCASIAN STANDS READY, ARMED WITH AN INCISIVE WIT

139

About the Authaz

Throckmorton "Monster" Monroe, Montgomery "Boot Knocka" Milkmoore III, and Frazier "IceCap" Van Helmanns first met as roommates at Harvard, where the three shared a fondness for early R&B artists.

Plagued by white liberal guilt, the three wrote, directed, and financed a traveling ice show entitled "Soul on Ice." Unfortunately, the first performance proved the project to be financially impractical. This, combined with a lawsuit from ex–Black Panther Eldridge Cleaver, killed any idea of follow-up performances.

Next, the three wrote and performed an original three-man musical entitled *Talking About Mother Africa,* which they presented on the Harvard campus. It was coolly received.

Undeterred, the three began spending the majority of their free time on the street corners and blues bars of predominantly black districts, where they studied the art of "the dozens," taking copious notes on their laptops and referring back to them at the dorm room. They would sometimes stay up all night honing their craft, quaffing cocktails, and listening to classical music.

After graduation, inspired by the film *White Men Can't Jump,* the group tried their hands at "free-style snapping" with locals on the basketball courts of Venice Beach. This endeavor was snuffed when they were hurt very badly. Bitter and resentful, the trio then set out to "prove" that the dozens were indeed an invention of the white man. This compilation is the culmination of their research.

Yes, that's right. Purchase The White Bread Snaps CD.

This handsome Certificate of Deposit matures in six months, two years, or even five. And emblazoned on its face are the favorite white bread snaps that you have grown to love. Carry the CD with you at all times— to the bank, to the country club, even the Junior Service League meetings—and get ready to throw down whenever some smart aleck starts playing the dozens with you.